MW01488471

Cooking Kids!

Jennifer L. Kingham

Writers Club Press
New York Lincoln Shanghai

Cooking Kids!

Writers Club Press
an imprint of iUniverse, Inc.

For information address:
iUniverse
2021 Pine Lake Road, Suite 100
Lincoln, NE 68512
www.iuniverse.com

ISBN: 0-595-25815-8 (Pbk)
ISBN: 0-595-65355-3 (Cloth)

Printed in the United States of America

For Taylor and Max
With Much, Much Love!

Acknowledgements

To my recipe testers, Chris Kingham, Darlene Brawner, Leanna Kingham, Gaylyn Haynes, and Christine Marler—thank you for your time and valuable feedback!!

Contents

Introduction

This cookbook was created for kids of all ages! Some recipes are easier than others, while some require parent's assistance, and others require a parent's watchful eye!

When cooking, feel free to experiment with the ingredients to create your own "invention". After each recipe section, there are pages for you to write down your own favorite recipes!

Cooking is a learning experience for a child and is a great activity for families as well as siblings.

ONE...

Before you start cooking...

☞ Tell your parent or an adult what you plan to cook.

☞ Before you starting cooking, always wash your hands.

☞ Read the recipe and make sure you have all the ingredients. It is helpful to place everything you need on the counter top.

☞ Each recipe tells you how long it takes to get the food ready and how long it takes to cook.

☞ Each recipe tells you how many servings the recipe will make. For example, if you see two 🍴🍴 symbols, the recipe will make enough for two kids.

☞ Always wash your hands after handling raw meat or eggs.

☞ Part of cooking is also cleaning up afterwards. Remember to leave the kitchen as you found it!

Two...

Parent Help...

⚇ At the top of each page, the Parent Help symbol ⚇ will be under the recipe name. All recipes will display one symbol ⚇ to remind you to always tell your parent or an adult that you plan to cook. If you see two symbols ⚇⚇, a parent or an adult needs to be in the kitchen with you in case you need help. If you see three symbols ⚇⚇⚇, a parent or an adult needs to help you.

THREE...GO!

Congratulations, you are ready to start cooking!

And don't forget to tell your parent or an adult!

Breakfast...

Snowman Pancakes
French Toast Cutters
Max's Muffins
Hamovers
Wafflo's

Snowman Pancakes

Prep Time: 10 minutes
Cook Time: 8 minutes
Total time until you can eat: 18 minutes

What you need:

- ✓ Medium mixing bowl
- ✓ Large Spoon
- ✓ Spatula
- ✓ Griddle or electric skillet
- ✓ Microwave
- ✓ Small bowl
- ✓ Measuring cups and spoons
- ✓ Butter knife

Ingredients:

- ✎ 1¼ cups flour
- ✎ 1 tablespoon sugar
- ✎ ¾ teaspoon salt
- ✎ 2½ teaspoons baking powder
- ✎ 3 tablespoons melted butter
- ✎ 1 cup milk
- ✎ 1 egg
- ✎ 1 bag of Mini M&M's

Directions:

- Preheat griddle or electric skillet to 250 degrees.
- Melt butter in a small bowl in the microwave for 30 seconds.
- Add eggs, milk, and melted butter to a medium mixing bowl.
- Stir until mixed thoroughly.
- Add flour, salt, sugar, and baking powder to the mixture.
- Stir until smooth and creamy.
- Dip the 1 tablespoon into the batter. Then, pour onto griddle or electric skillet to form the head of the snowman.
- Dip the ¼ measuring cup into the batter. Then, pour onto griddle or electric skillet next to the head to form the mid section of the snowman.
- Dip the ¼ measuring cup into the batter. Then, pour onto griddle or electric skillet next to the mid section to form the bottom of the snowman.
- Repeat the above three steps to make another snowman.
- After 2 two minutes, carefully flip the snowman pancake using a spatula.
- Cook for two minutes then carefully place both snowmen on a plate using a spatula.
- Repeat the above five steps to make two more pancakes.
- Decorate each snowman with Mini M&M's for the eyes, nose, mouth, and buttons.

Serve with lots of butter and syrup!

French Toast Cutters

Prep Time: 10 minutes
Cook Time: 8 minutes
Total time until you can eat: 18 minutes

What you need:

- ✓ Medium mixing bowl
- ✓ A griddle or electric skillet
- ✓ Spatula
- ✓ Fork
- ✓ Measuring cups and spoons
- ✓ Favorite cookie cutters

Ingredients:

- 8 pieces of sandwich bread
- 4 eggs
- 1 cup milk
- 1 teaspoon vanilla
- 1 tablespoon sugar
- ½ teaspoon salt
- ¼ cup powdered sugar
- Pam non-stick cooking spray

Directions:

- ● Preheat griddle or electric skillet to 250 degrees.
- ● Add eggs, milk, vanilla, salt, and sugar to the mixing bowl.
- ● Stir ingredients together with a fork until blended.
- ● Using your favorite cookie cutter, press the cookie cutter into each piece of bread. Remove the excess bread.
- ● When the griddle or electric skillet is heated (approximately 5 minutes), spray non-stick spray onto the surface.
- ● Dip a piece of bread into the mixture. Make sure both sides are completely covered with the mixture.
- ● Place the bread onto the griddle or electric skillet.
- ● Repeat the above two steps for each piece of bread (cook 4 pieces of bread at the same time).
- ● After two minutes, use a spatula to turn the bread over. Cook 2 minutes.
- ● Using the spatula, place the toast on plates.
- ● Repeat the above five steps for the remaining 4 slices of bread.
- ● Using your fingers, sprinkle powdered sugar on top of each piece of French toast.

Serve with plenty of syrup!

Max's Muffins

🧒🧒🧒

🍽 X 12

Prep Time: 10 minutes
Cook Time: 30 minutes
Total time until you can eat: 55 minutes

What you need:

- ✓ Oven
- ✓ Medium mixing bowl
- ✓ Muffin pan
- ✓ Spoon
- ✓ 12 paper cupcake holders
- ✓ Potholders

Ingredients:

- 1 cup milk
- ½ cup olive oil
- 1½ cup flour
- ½ cup sugar
- 3 teaspoons baking powder
- ½ teaspoon salt
- ¾ cup mini chocolate chips
- Pam non-stick cooking spray

Directions:

- Preheat oven to 400 degrees.
- In the medium mixing bowl, add milk and olive oil.
- Stir until blended.
- Add flour, sugar, baking powder, and salt.
- Stir until blended.
- Add mini chocolate chips.
- Stir until blended.
- Place paper cupcake holders into the muffin pan holes.
- Spray Pam non-stick cooking spray into each paper holder to evenly coat.
- Scoop approximately three spoonfuls of batter into each holder. Repeat 11 times to fill each holder.
- Place the muffin pan in the oven and set the timer for 30 minutes.
- Using potholders, remove the muffin pan from the oven and turn off the oven.
- Let cool for 15 minutes.

Serve with heaps of butter!

Hamovers

Prep Time: 10 minutes
Cook Time: 10 minutes
Total time until you can eat: 22 minutes

What you need:

- ✓ Cookie sheet
- ✓ Rolling pin
- ✓ Butter knife
- ✓ Spatula
- ✓ Potholders

Ingredients:

- ✎ 8 slices of ham sliced thin or shaved
- ✎ 4 slices of American cheese
- ✎ 1 can of biscuits

Directions:

- Preheat oven to 425 degrees.
- Place biscuits on the countertop (approximately 2 inches apart).
- Using the rolling pin, flatten each biscuit until twice the size of the original biscuit.
- Place the flattened biscuits on to a cookie sheet.
- Cut each slice of cheese in half.
- Place 1 half of a slice of American cheese on each biscuit.
- Place 1 piece of ham (folded in half) on each biscuit.
- Fold each biscuit in half. Press the sides down so the cheese does not leak out when melted.
- Place the cookie sheet in the oven.
- Set the timer for 10 minutes.
- Using a potholder, remove the cookie sheet from the oven after 10 minutes or until golden brown.
- Place cookie sheet on a potholder and let the turnovers cool approximately 2 minutes.
- Turn off the oven.
- Using the spatula, remove the turnovers from the cookie sheet on to plates.

Serve with mustard!

Wafflo's

Prep Time: 15 minutes
Cook Time: 5 minutes (for each)
Total time until you can eat: 20 minutes

What you need:

- ✓ 2 Small mixing bowls
- ✓ Medium mixing bowl
- ✓ A griddle or electric skillet
- ✓ Microwave
- ✓ Electric Mixer
- ✓ Spoon
- ✓ Spatula
- ✓ Measuring cups and spoons
- ✓ Small pitcher

Ingredients:

- ☞ 2 eggs
- ☞ 1 2/3 cups milk
- ☞ 4 tablespoons butter
- ☞ 2 cups flour
- ☞ 1 tablespoon sugar
- ☞ ½ teaspoon salt
- ☞ 4 teaspoons baking powder

Directions:

- Preheat waffle iron.
- Break eggs and separate the whites into the small bowl and the yolks into the medium bowl.
- Using the electric mixer, beat egg whites until soft peaks (this means when you stop mixing gently pull the beaters straight up and a "peak" will form).
- In the other small mixing bowl, melt butter in the microwave for 30 seconds.
- In the medium bowl with the egg yolks, add milk and melted butter.
- Blend with the electric mixer until smooth.
- Add flour, sugar, salt, and baking powder to the medium bowl.
- Blend with the electric mixer until smooth.
- With the spatula, pour egg whites into batter and fold (this means to gently stir egg whites in a circler motion starting from the top down to the bottom) until blended.
- Pour batter into the pitcher.
- Slowly pour batter onto the waffle iron until all holes are filled.
- Cook waffle approximately 5 minutes or until golden brown.
- Repeat the above two steps three times.
- Using a fork, carefully remove the waffles from the iron and place on a plate.
- Unplug the waffle iron.

Serve with oodles of butter (or peanut butter) and syrup!

Your Own Breakfast Recipes!

Here are pages for you to write your own breakfast recipes!

🐣 Don't forget to tell your parents or an adult that you plan to cook!

✓ For each recipe, gather all the kitchen utensils, bowls, potholders, etc. that you need for your "invention". Use the area labeled "What you need" to write down the items you gathered for the recipe.

🖋 Next, gather all the ingredients you need to make your recipe. Use the area labeled "Ingredients" to write down all the ingredients you gathered.

🍴 Finally, start cooking! After each step you take while you are cooking, write down what you just did in the area labeled "Directions".

Congratulations! You just wrote your own recipe. You just invented something!

Your Own Breakfast Recipes!

Recipe Name_____

What you need

✓ _____
✓ _____
✓ _____
✓ _____
✓ _____
✓ _____
✓ _____
✓ _____

Ingredients

✒ _____
✒ _____
✒ _____
✒ _____
✒ _____
✒ _____
✒ _____
✒ _____
✒ _____
✒ _____
✒ _____

Your Own Breakfast Recipes!

Directions

🗣_____
🗣_____
🗣_____
🗣_____
🗣_____
🗣_____
🗣_____
🗣_____
🗣_____
🗣_____
🗣_____
🗣_____
🗣_____
🗣_____
🗣_____

Your Own Breakfast Recipes!

Recipe Name_____

What you need
✓ _____
✓ _____
✓ _____
✓ _____
✓ _____
✓ _____
✓ _____
✓ _____

Ingredients
✍ _____
✍ _____
✍ _____
✍ _____
✍ _____
✍ _____
✍ _____
✍ _____
✍ _____
✍ _____
✍ _____

Your Own Breakfast Recipes!

Directions

Your Own Breakfast Recipes!

Recipe Name_____

What you need

✓ _____
✓ _____
✓ _____
✓ _____
✓ _____
✓ _____
✓ _____
✓ _____

Ingredients

✐ _____
✐ _____
✐ _____
✐ _____
✐ _____
✐ _____
✐ _____
✐ _____
✐ _____
✐ _____
✐ _____

Your Own Breakfast Recipes!

Directions

_____
_____
_____
_____
_____
_____
_____
_____
_____
_____
_____
_____
_____
_____
_____

Your Own Breakfast Recipes!

Recipe Name_____

What you need
✓ _____
✓ _____
✓ _____
✓ _____
✓ _____
✓ _____
✓ _____
✓ _____

Ingredients
✐ _____
✐ _____
✐ _____
✐ _____
✐ _____
✐ _____
✐ _____
✐ _____
✐ _____
✐ _____
✐ _____
✐ _____

Your Own Breakfast Recipes!

Directions

🗣_____
🗣_____
🗣_____
🗣_____
🗣_____
🗣_____
🗣_____
🗣_____
🗣_____
🗣_____
🗣_____
🗣_____
🗣_____
🗣_____
🗣_____

Your Own Breakfast Recipes!

Recipe Name_____

What you need
✓ _____
✓ _____
✓ _____
✓ _____
✓ _____
✓ _____
✓ _____
✓ _____

Ingredients
✒ _____
✒ _____
✒ _____
✒ _____
✒ _____
✒ _____
✒ _____
✒ _____
✒ _____
✒ _____
✒ _____

Your Own Breakfast Recipes!

Directions

🗣_____

🗣_____

🗣_____

🗣_____

🗣_____

🗣_____

🗣_____

🗣_____

🗣_____

🗣_____

🗣_____

🗣_____

🗣_____

🗣_____

🗣_____

Lunch...

Cheesidillas
Cheesy Broccoli Soup
Mac and Cheese Please
Hammer's
Mini Pizza

Cheesidillas

Prep Time: 5 minutes
Cook Time: 10 minutes
Total time until you can eat: 17 minutes

What you need:

✓   Large Cookie sheet
✓   Serrated knife or pizza cutter
✓   Measuring cups and spoons
✓   Potholders

Ingredients:

☛   8 soft taco size flour tortillas
☛   1 cup grated cheddar cheese
☛   1 cup grated monterey jack cheese
☛   1 teaspoon garlic powder
☛   1 teaspoon cumin powder
☛   Pam non-stick cooking spray

Directions:

- Preheat the oven for 350 degrees.
- Arrange four flour tortillas on a large cookie sheet.
- Sprinkle ¼ cup cheddar cheese on each tortilla.
- Sprinkle ¼ cup Monterey Jack cheese on each tortilla.
- Sprinkle ¼ teaspoon of garlic powder on each tortilla.
- Sprinkle ¼ teaspoon cumin on each tortilla.
- Place the remaining flour tortillas on top of each tortilla.
- Spray Pam on the top of each tortilla.
- Place the cookie sheet in the oven.
- Set the timer for 10 minutes.
- After 10 minutes, remove the cookie sheet and place on a potholder to cool for 2 minutes.
- Turn off the oven.
- Cut each tortilla into four sections (cut in half then in half again) with a knife or pizza cutter.

Serve with mounds of sour cream and salsa!

Cheesy Broccoli Soup

Prep Time: 5 minutes
Cook Time: 30 minutes
Total time until you can eat: 35 minutes

What you need:

✓ Blender
✓ Steamer
✓ Serrated knife
✓ Potholders
✓ Quart size saucepan
✓ Spoon
✓ Measuring cups and spoons

Ingredients:

✎ 2 cups raw broccoli flowerettes
✎ 2 cups milk
✎ 8 ounces of Velveeta cheese (1 cup cubed)
✎ ¼ cup grated Parmesan cheese

Directions:

- Wash broccoli and cut into flowerettes (cut off the stems).
- Fill the steamer with water following the steamer's directions.
- Place the broccoli in the steamer and steam for 15 minutes following the steamer's directions.
- Cut the Velveeta cheese into cubes.
- Place the sauce plan on the stove burner and turn on low heat.
- Add 2 cups of milk to the saucepan.
- Add Velveeta cheese and stir occasionally until the cheese melts.
- Turn the burner off and place the saucepan on a potholder.
- Once the broccoli is steamed, drain the broccoli and add to blender.
- Pour the cheese sauce into the blender.
- Blend for 1 minute or until creamy.
- Pour soup into three bowls and sprinkle Parmesan cheese on top.

Serve with tons of crackers!

Mac and Cheese Please

Prep Time: 5 minutes
Cook Time: 14 minutes
Total time until you can eat: 19 minutes

What you need:

✓   Quart sauce pan and lid
✓   Spoon
✓   Serrated knife
✓   Measuring cups
✓   Colander
✓   Potholders

Ingredients:

☛   2 cups of your favorite pasta noodles
☛   3 cups water
☛   1 cup cubed Velveeta cheese
☛   ¼ cup milk
☛   ¼ cup of grated Parmesan cheese

Directions:

- Place sauce pan on a burner and turn on medium high heat.
- Add 2 cups of water to the pan.
- When water boils, add pasta and stir.
- Turn the burner to low and cover pan with the lid.
- Set the timer for 12 minutes.
- Cut the Velveeta into cubes.
- After 12 minutes, turn off burner.
- Place the colander in the sink.
- Using a potholder, remove the lid and pour pasta into colander to drain the water.
- Once drained, pour the pasta back into the pan.
- Place the pan on the burner.
- Add Velveeta cubes and milk.
- Turn the burner on low.
- Stir occasionally until the cheese is melted.
- Turn off burner and add Mac and Cheese to bowls.
- Sprinkle Parmesan cheese on top of the Mac and Cheese.

Serve with warm, buttery bread!

Hammer's

Prep Time: 7 minutes
Cook Time: 0 minutes
Total time until you can eat: 7 minutes

What you need:

✓   Butter knife

Ingredients:

- 3 soft taco size flour tortillas
- 3 tablespoons of cream cheese spread
- ¾ teaspoon garlic powder
- 6 slices of shaved or thinly sliced ham
- 6 slices of thinly sliced mozzarella cheese

Directions:

- Spread 1 tablespoon of cream cheese evenly on each tortilla.
- Sprinkle ¼ teaspoon of garlic powder on each tortilla.
- Place 2 pieces of ham on each tortilla.
- Place 2 pieces of mozzarella cheese on each tortilla.
- Roll each tortilla into a burrito and place on a plate.

Serve with crispy chips or crackers!

Mini Pizza

Prep Time: 5 minutes
Cook Time: 10 minutes
Total time until you can eat: 17 minutes

What you need:

✓ Serrated knife
✓ Oven
✓ Cookie sheet
✓ Can opener
✓ Measuring cups and spoons
✓ Spatula
✓ Potholders

Ingredients:

✎ 2 plain English muffins
✎ ¼ cup of an 8 ounce can of Hunt's Oregano, Basil, and Garlic Tomato sauce
✎ ½ cup of shredded mozzarella cheese
✎ 20 slices of pepperoni

Directions:

- Preheat the oven for 400 degrees.
- Cut the English muffins in half and place on a cookie sheet.
- Spread 1 tablespoon of sauce on each half.
- Sprinkle 1/8 cup of cheese on each half.
- Place 5 slices of pepperoni on each half.
- Place the cookie sheet in the oven and set the timer for 10 minutes.
- After 10 minutes using a potholder, remove the cookie sheet and turn off the oven.
- Using a spatula, place the halves on plates.
- Let cool for 2 minutes.

Top with Parmesan cheese and serve Ranch dressing for dipping!

Your Own Lunch Recipes!

Here are pages for you to write your own breakfast recipes!

☻ Don't forget to tell your parents or an adult that you plan to cook!

✓ For each recipe, gather all the kitchen utensils, bowls, potholders, etc. that you need for your "invention". Use the area labeled "What you need" to write down the items you gathered for the recipe.

✎ Next, gather all the ingredients you need to make your recipe. Use the area labeled "Ingredients" to write down all the ingredients you gathered.

♠ Finally, start cooking! After each step you take while you are cooking, write down what you just did in the area labeled "Directions".

Congratulations! You just wrote your own recipe. You just invented something!

Your Own Lunch Recipes!

Recipe Name_____

What you need
✓ _____
✓ _____
✓ _____
✓ _____
✓ _____
✓ _____
✓ _____
✓ _____

Ingredients
✐ _____
✐ _____
✐ _____
✐ _____
✐ _____
✐ _____
✐ _____
✐ _____
✐ _____
✐ _____
✐ _____

Your Own Lunch Recipes!

Directions

❧_____
❧_____
❧_____
❧_____
❧_____
❧_____
❧_____
❧_____
❧_____
❧_____
❧_____
❧_____
❧_____
❧_____
❧_____

Your Own Lunch Recipes!

Recipe Name_____

What you need

✓ _____
✓ _____
✓ _____
✓ _____
✓ _____
✓ _____
✓ _____
✓ _____

Ingredients

✐ _____
✐ _____
✐ _____
✐ _____
✐ _____
✐ _____
✐ _____
✐ _____
✐ _____
✐ _____
✐ _____

Your Own Lunch Recipes!

Directions

_____
_____
_____
_____
_____
_____
_____
_____
_____
_____
_____
_____
_____
_____
_____

Your Own Lunch Recipes!

Recipe Name_____

What you need

✓ _____
✓ _____
✓ _____
✓ _____
✓ _____
✓ _____
✓ _____
✓ _____

Ingredients

✐ _____
✐ _____
✐ _____
✐ _____
✐ _____
✐ _____
✐ _____
✐ _____
✐ _____
✐ _____
✐ _____

Your Own Lunch Recipes!

Directions

🤚_____
🤚_____
🤚_____
🤚_____
🤚_____
🤚_____
🤚_____
🤚_____
🤚_____
🤚_____
🤚_____
🤚_____
🤚_____
🤚_____
🤚_____

Your Own Lunch Recipes!

Recipe Name_____

What you need
✓ _____
✓ _____
✓ _____
✓ _____
✓ _____
✓ _____
✓ _____
✓ _____

Ingredients
✒ _____
✒ _____
✒ _____
✒ _____
✒ _____
✒ _____
✒ _____
✒ _____
✒ _____
✒ _____
✒ _____

Your Own Lunch Recipes!

Directions

- _____
- _____
- _____
- _____
- _____
- _____
- _____
- _____
- _____
- _____
- _____
- _____
- _____
- _____
- _____

Your Own Lunch Recipes!

Recipe Name_____

What you need

✓ _____
✓ _____
✓ _____
✓ _____
✓ _____
✓ _____
✓ _____
✓ _____

Ingredients

✐ _____
✐ _____
✐ _____
✐ _____
✐ _____
✐ _____
✐ _____
✐ _____
✐ _____
✐ _____
✐ _____

Your Own Lunch Recipes!

Directions

_____

_____

_____

_____

_____

_____

_____

_____

_____

_____

_____

_____

_____

_____

_____

Snacks...

Art Dip
Rainbow Dip
Dreamy Dip and Fruit
Graham Cookies
Taylor's Tortilla Jams

Art Dip

Prep Time: 35 minutes
Cook Time: 20 minutes
Total time until you can eat: 1 hour and 1 minute

What you need:

- ✓ Oven
- ✓ 9 x 12 baking dish
- ✓ Medium mixing bowl
- ✓ Spoon
- ✓ Electric mixer
- ✓ Measuring cups and spoons
- ✓ Can opener
- ✓ Potholders

Ingredients:

- ✒ 2 8 ounce packages of cream cheese
- ✒ 1 tablespoon all purpose seasoning
- ✒ 1 14 ounce can of small artichoke hearts
- ✒ ¼ cup grated Parmesan cheese

Directions:

- Set the cream cheese on the countertop 30 minutes before making the recipe.
- Preheat oven for 350 degrees.
- Open the can of artichokes and drain the liquid.
- Place the artichokes in the mixing bowl.
- Mix the artichoke hearts with the electric mixer for 1 minute.
- Add the cream cheese and 1 tablespoon of all-purpose seasoning to the bowl.
- Mix with the electric mixer until smooth.
- Scoop dip into the baking dish.
- Place baking dish in the oven and set the timer for 20 minutes.
- After 20 minutes using the potholder, remove baking dish from the oven and place on a potholder.
- Sprinkle Parmesan cheese evenly onto the dip.
- Place the baking dish back into the oven.
- Turn the oven on broil and set the timer for 1 minute.
- Using the potholder, remove the baking dish from the oven and place on another potholder.
- Turn off the oven.
- Let cool for 5 minutes.

Serve with your favorite tortilla chips or crackers!

Rainbow Dip

Prep Time: 10 minutes
Cook Time: 0 minutes
Total time until you can eat: 10 minutes

What you need:

✓ Can opener
✓ Small mixing bowl
✓ Spoon
✓ 9X12 baking dish
✓ Measuring cups

Ingredients:

⚲ 1 16 ounce can of refried beans
⚲ 1 package of taco seasoning
⚲ 1 16 ounce container of sour cream
⚲ 1 16 ounce container of guacamole
⚲ 1 16 ounce jar of salsa
⚲ 1 cup shredded cheddar cheese
⚲ 1 cup shredded monterey jack cheese

Directions:

- In a small mixing bowl, add the refried beans.
- Add the taco seasoning and stir until blended.
- Spoon the bean mixture into the 9X12 baking dish and spread evenly.
- Spoon the sour cream over the bean mixture and spread evenly.
- Spoon the guacamole over the sour cream and spread evenly.
- Spoon the salsa over the guacamole and spread evenly.
- Evenly sprinkle the cheddar cheese over the guacamole.
- Evenly sprinkle the monterey jack cheese over the cheddar cheese.

Serve with muchos chips!

Dreamy Dip & Fruit

🍴 🍴 🍴 🍴 🍴 🍴

Prep Time: 1 hour and 10 minutes
Cook Time: 0 minutes
Total time until you can eat: 1 hour and 10 minutes

What you need:

✓ Medium mixing bowl
✓ Small serving bowl
✓ Spoon
✓ Serrated Knife
✓ Plate
✓ Toothpicks

Ingredients:

✐ 1 8 ounce package cream cheese
✐ 1 7 ounce jar of marshmallow cream
✐ 1 banana
✐ 1 apple
✐ 1 pint of strawberries
✐ 1 cup grapes

Directions:

- Place cream cheese on countertop 1 hour before preparing snack to soften.
- Once softened, place the cream cheese and marshmallow cream in a medium mixing bowl.
- Stir until mixed thoroughly.
- Spoon the mixture into a small serving bowl.
- Peel the banana and slice.
- Slice the apples.
- Cut the top of the strawberries.
- Add the bananas, apples, strawberries, and grapes to the plate.
- Stick the toothpicks into each piece of fruit.

Eat!

Graham Cookies

Prep Time: 5 minutes
Cook Time: 0 minutes
Total time until you can eat: 5 minutes

What you need:

✓ Butter knife
✓ Measuring spoons

Ingredients:

- 4 chocolate graham crackers
- 2 tablespoons of peanut butter
- 2 tablespoons mini chocolate chips
- 4 teaspoons Caramel sauce

Directions:

- Break the chocolate graham crackers in half so you will have four pieces.
- Spread ½ tablespoon of peanut butter on each piece.
- Sprinkle ½ tablespoon of mini chocolate chips on each piece.
- Drizzle 1 teaspoon of Caramel sauce on top of each piece over the chocolate chips.
- Place on a plate.

Serve with ice, cold milk!

Taylor's Tortilla Jams

Prep Time: 5 minutes
Cook Time: 0 minutes
Total time until you can eat: 5 minutes

What you need:

✓ Butter knife
✓ Plate
✓ Measuring spoons

Ingredients:

✎ 4 soft taco size flour tortillas
✎ 4 tablespoons of cream cheese spread
✎ 4 tablespoons of strawberry jam (or your favorite jam!)

Directions:

- Spread 1 tablespoon of cream cheese on each tortilla.
- Spread 1 tablespoon of jam on top of the cream cheese on each tortilla.
- Fold and roll each tortilla into a burrito.
- Place tortillas on a plate.

Eat!

Your Own Snack Recipes!

Here are pages for you to write your own breakfast recipes!

Don't forget to tell your parents or an adult that you plan to cook!

✓ For each recipe, gather all the kitchen utensils, bowls, potholders, etc. that you need for your "invention". Use the area labeled "What you need" to write down the items you gathered for the recipe.

Next, gather all the ingredients you need to make your recipe. Use the area labeled "Ingredients" to write down all the ingredients you gathered.

Finally, start cooking! After each step you take while you are cooking, write down what you just did in the area labeled "Directions".

Congratulations! You just wrote your own recipe. You just invented something!

Your Own Snack Recipes!

Recipe Name_____

What you need
✓ _____
✓ _____
✓ _____
✓ _____
✓ _____
✓ _____
✓ _____
✓ _____

Ingredients
✐ _____
✐ _____
✐ _____
✐ _____
✐ _____
✐ _____
✐ _____
✐ _____
✐ _____
✐ _____
✐ _____

Your Own Snack Recipes!

Directions

_____

_____

_____

_____

_____

_____

_____

_____

_____

_____

_____

_____

_____

_____

_____

Your Own Snack Recipes!

Recipe Name_____

What you need
✓ _____
✓ _____
✓ _____
✓ _____
✓ _____
✓ _____
✓ _____
✓ _____

Ingredients
✐ _____
✐ _____
✐ _____
✐ _____
✐ _____
✐ _____
✐ _____
✐ _____
✐ _____
✐ _____
✐ _____

Your Own Snack Recipes!

Directions

❖_____
❖_____
❖_____
❖_____
❖_____
❖_____
❖_____
❖_____
❖_____
❖_____
❖_____
❖_____
❖_____
❖_____
❖_____

Your Own Snack Recipes!

Recipe Name_____

What you need
✓ _____
✓ _____
✓ _____
✓ _____
✓ _____
✓ _____
✓ _____
✓ _____

Ingredients
✒ _____
✒ _____
✒ _____
✒ _____
✒ _____
✒ _____
✒ _____
✒ _____
✒ _____
✒ _____
✒ _____

Your Own Snack Recipes!

Directions

🖐_____

🖐_____

🖐_____

🖐_____

🖐_____

🖐_____

🖐_____

🖐_____

🖐_____

🖐_____

🖐_____

🖐_____

🖐_____

🖐_____

Your Own Snack Recipes!

Recipe Name_____

What you need

✓ _____
✓ _____
✓ _____
✓ _____
✓ _____
✓ _____
✓ _____
✓ _____

Ingredients

➤ _____
➤ _____
➤ _____
➤ _____
➤ _____
➤ _____
➤ _____
➤ _____
➤ _____
➤ _____
➤ _____

Your Own Snack Recipes!

Directions

❧_____

❧_____

❧_____

❧_____

❧_____

❧_____

❧_____

❧_____

❧_____

❧_____

❧_____

❧_____

❧_____

❧_____

❧_____

Your Own Snack Recipes!

Recipe Name_____

What you need

✓ _____

✓ _____

✓ _____

✓ _____

✓ _____

✓ _____

✓ _____

✓ _____

Ingredients

✐ _____

✐ _____

✐ _____

✐ _____

✐ _____

✐ _____

✐ _____

✐ _____

✐ _____

✐ _____

✐ _____

Your Own Snack Recipes!

Directions

_____

_____

_____

_____

_____

_____

_____

_____

_____

_____

_____

_____

_____

_____

_____

Dinner...

Meatloaf Surprise
Cheesy Chicken
Tuna Fish Gravy
Baked Burritos
Cheesy Burgers

Meatloaf Surprise

Prep Time: 12 minutes
Cook Time: 1 hour
Total time until you can eat: 1 hour and 17 minutes

What you need:

✓   Oven
✓   Measuring cups and spoons
✓   Loaf pan baking dish
✓   Spoon
✓   Medium mixing bowl
✓   Potholders

Ingredients:

☛   1 pound ground beef
☛   ¼ cup ketchup
☛   1 package Lipton Mushroom Onion Soup Mix
☛   3 tablespoons Worcestershire
☛   ½ cup water
☛   2/3 cup breadcrumbs
☛   Pam non-stick cooking spray

Directions:

- Preheat oven for 350 degrees.
- Add ketchup, soup mix, 2 tablespoons Worcestershire, water, and breadcrumbs into mixing bowl.
- Stir until thoroughly mixed.
- Add ground beef and mix together using your hands!
- Spray loaf pan with Pam.
- Place the meatloaf mixture into loaf pan.
- Form mixture into a loaf.
- Pour 1 tablespoon Worcestershire on top of the meatloaf.
- Place in the oven and set the timer for 1 hour.
- After an hour using a potholder, remove the meatloaf from the oven and let cool for 5 minutes.
- Turn off the oven.
- Slice and place on plates.

Serve with lots of ketchup, bread, and your favorite veggies!!!

Cheesy Chicken

Prep Time: 12 minutes
Cook Time: 30 minutes
Total time until you can eat: 47 minutes

What you need:

✓ Oven
✓ 9x12 baking dish
✓ Serrated knife
✓ Small mixing bowl
✓ Plate
✓ Fork
✓ Measuring cups and spoons
✓ Potholders

Ingredients:

➤ 1 cup milk
➤ 1 egg
➤ 2 cups grated Parmesan cheese
➤ ½ teaspoon garlic powder
➤ 4 chicken breasts
➤ Pam non-stick cooking spray

Directions:

- Preheat oven for 400 degrees.
- Add egg and milk to a small mixing bowl.
- Stir until mixed.
- Add Parmesan cheese to the plate.
- Spray Pam onto the baking dish.
- Dip each chicken breast into the milk mixture then place onto the Parmesan cheese.
- Turn the chicken over to evenly coat both sides with Parmesan cheese. Repeat with each chicken breast.
- Place chicken into the baking dish.
- Sprinkle each piece evenly with garlic powder.
- Place the baking dish in the oven and set the timer for 30 minutes.
- After 30 minutes using a potholder, remove the baking dish from the oven.
- Turn off the oven.
- Let cool for 5 minutes.
- Place the chicken onto plates.

Serve with bread and your favorite veggies or pasta!

Tuna Fish Gravy

Prep Time: 5 minutes
Cook Time: 10 minutes
Total time until you can eat: 15 minutes

What you need:

✓ Skillet
✓ Fork
✓ Spoon
✓ Butter knife
✓ Measuring cups and spoons
✓ Toaster
✓ Potholder

Ingredients:

- 3 3 ounce cans of Albacore Tuna
- 3 tablespoons butter
- 4 tablespoons flour
- 2 cups milk
- ½ teaspoon salt
- 6 slices of bread

Directions:

- Place skillet on the burner and turn on medium heat.
- Add butter and melt.
- Add flour and stir.
- Slowly add milk and stir until smooth.
- Open the cans of tuna and drain the liquid.
- Add the tuna to the mixture.
- Add salt and stir until smooth.
- Toast bread in toaster and place on a plate.
- Turn off the burner.
- Using a potholder, pour the Tuna Fish Gravy over the toasted bread.

Serve with warm Baby LeSeur peas!

Baked Burritos

Prep Time: 10 minutes
Cook Time: 15 minutes
Total time until you can eat: 27 minutes

What you need:

- ✓ Oven
- ✓ Butter Knife
- ✓ Can Opener
- ✓ Measuring cups and spoons
- ✓ 6X9 Baking dish
- ✓ 2 small mixing bowls
- ✓ Spoon
- ✓ Spatula
- ✓ Potholders

Ingredients:

- 1 16 ounce can of refried beans
- 1 cup grated cheddar cheese
- 1 cup grated monterey jack cheese
- 4 burrito size flour tortillas
- 1 4 ounce can of chopped green chilies
- ½ teaspoon Fajita seasoning
- Pam non-stick cooking spray

Directions:

- Preheat oven to 400 degrees.
- In the small mixing bowl, add the refried beans, green chilies, garlic, and Fajita seasoning.
- Stir until blended.
- In the other small mixing bowl, add both cheeses and toss together using your hands.
- Spray the baking dish with Pam non-stick cooking spray.
- Spoon ¼ of the bean mixture into each tortilla.
- Spoon 1/3 cup of the cheese mixture into each tortilla.
- Roll each tortilla into a burrito and place in the baking dish.
- Sprinkle the remainder of the cheese mixture on top of the burritos.
- Place the baking dish in the oven and set the timer for 15 minutes.
- After 15 minutes using a potholder, remove the baking dish from the oven.
- Turn off the oven.
- Let cool for 2 minutes.
- Using the spatula, place the burritos onto plates.

Serve with zesty salsa and sour cream!

Cheesy Burgers

Prep Time: 10 minutes
Cook Time: 16 minutes
Total time until you can eat: 26 minutes

What you need:

✓ Large Skillet
✓ 9x12 baking dish
✓ Spatula
✓ Measuring cups and spoons

Ingredients:

✎ 1 pound ground beef
✎ ½ cup Parmesan cheese
✎ 1 tablespoon all purpose seasoning
✎ 4 teaspoons Worcestershire
✎ 4 hamburger buns
✎ 4 slices of American cheese
✎ 4 slices of Swiss cheese

Directions:

- In a small mixing bowl, add the ground beef, Parmesan cheese, and the all purpose seasoning.
- Using your hands, mix thoroughly.
- Make 4 hamburger patties from the ground beef and place into baking dish.
- Pour 1 teaspoon Worcestershire on each patty.
- Place the skillet onto the burner and turn on medium heat.
- Heat skillet for 2 minutes.
- Using a spatula, place the patties into the skillet.
- Cook patties for approximately 8 minutes on each side (To make sure they are done, cut one patty in half. If you see pink or red, cook until light brown in the middle of the patty).
- Turn off the burner.
- Using a spatula, place each patty on a hamburger bun.
- Add a slice of American and Swiss on top of each patty then top with a bun.

Serve with French Fries or Nachos and of course your favorite condiments!

Your Own Dinner Recipes!

Here are pages for you to write your own breakfast recipes!

🧒 Don't forget to tell your parents or an adult that you plan to cook!

✓ For each recipe, gather all the kitchen utensils, bowls, potholders, etc. that you need for your "invention". Use the area labeled "What you need" to write down the items you gathered for the recipe.

✐ Next, gather all the ingredients you need to make your recipe. Use the area labeled "Ingredients" to write down all the ingredients you gathered.

🥄 Finally, start cooking! After each step you take while you are cooking, write down what you just did in the area labeled "Directions".

Congratulations! You just wrote your own recipe. You just invented something!

Your Own Dinner Recipes!

Recipe Name_____

What you need

✓ _____
✓ _____
✓ _____
✓ _____
✓ _____
✓ _____
✓ _____
✓ _____

Ingredients

✐ _____
✐ _____
✐ _____
✐ _____
✐ _____
✐ _____
✐ _____
✐ _____
✐ _____
✐ _____
✐ _____

Your Own Dinner Recipes!

Directions

🤚_____

🤚_____

🤚_____

🤚_____

🤚_____

🤚_____

🤚_____

🤚_____

🤚_____

🤚_____

🤚_____

🤚_____

🤚_____

🤚_____

🤚_____

Your Own Dinner Recipes!

Recipe Name_____

What you need
✓ _____
✓ _____
✓ _____
✓ _____
✓ _____
✓ _____
✓ _____
✓ _____

Ingredients
✒ _____
✒ _____
✒ _____
✒ _____
✒ _____
✒ _____
✒ _____
✒ _____
✒ _____
✒ _____
✒ _____

Your Own Dinner Recipes!

Directions

✊_____
✊_____
✊_____
✊_____
✊_____
✊_____
✊_____
✊_____
✊_____
✊_____
✊_____
✊_____
✊_____
✊_____
✊_____

Your Own Dinner Recipes!

Recipe Name_____

What you need

✓ _____
✓ _____
✓ _____
✓ _____
✓ _____
✓ _____
✓ _____
✓ _____

Ingredients

✒ _____
✒ _____
✒ _____
✒ _____
✒ _____
✒ _____
✒ _____
✒ _____
✒ _____
✒ _____
✒ _____

Your Own Dinner Recipes!

Directions

❦_____
❦_____
❦_____
❦_____
❦_____
❦_____
❦_____
❦_____
❦_____
❦_____
❦_____
❦_____
❦_____
❦_____
❦_____

Your Own Dinner Recipes!

Recipe Name_____

What you need
✓ _____
✓ _____
✓ _____
✓ _____
✓ _____
✓ _____
✓ _____
✓ _____

Ingredients
➤ _____
➤ _____
➤ _____
➤ _____
➤ _____
➤ _____
➤ _____
➤ _____
➤ _____
➤ _____
➤ _____

Your Own Dinner Recipes!

Directions

👤‹ _____

👤‹ _____

👤‹ _____

👤‹ _____

👤‹ _____

👤‹ _____

👤‹ _____

👤‹ _____

👤‹ _____

👤‹ _____

👤‹ _____

👤‹ _____

👤‹ _____

👤‹ _____

👤‹ _____

Your Own Dinner Recipes!

Recipe Name_____

What you need
✓ _____
✓ _____
✓ _____
✓ _____
✓ _____
✓ _____
✓ _____
✓ _____

Ingredients
🖋 _____
🖋 _____
🖋 _____
🖋 _____
🖋 _____
🖋 _____
🖋 _____
🖋 _____
🖋 _____
🖋 _____
🖋 _____

Your Own Dinner Recipes!

Directions

🍴_____

🍴_____

🍴_____

🍴_____

🍴_____

🍴_____

🍴_____

🍴_____

🍴_____

🍴_____

🍴_____

🍴_____

🍴_____

🍴_____

🍴_____

Desserts...

Chocolate Chip Mousse
Ice Cream Cookies
Chocolate Chippers
Chocol-Shake
Smootheeee

Chocolate Chip Mousse

Prep Time: 6 minutes
Cook Time: 0 minutes
Total time until you can eat: 1 hour and 6 minutes

What you need:

- ✓ Large mixing bowl
- ✓ Spoon
- ✓ Measuring cups and spoons
- ✓ 6 Dessert bowls

Ingredients:

- ☛ 1 12 ounce container of Cool Whip
- ☛ 1 5.9 ounce package of Jell-O Instant Chocolate Pudding
- ☛ 1 cup milk
- ☛ 4 tablespoons mini semi-sweet chocolate chips

Directions:

- In the large mixing bowl, add the instant chocolate pudding mix, cool whip, and milk.
- Stir until thoroughly blended.
- Add 3 tablespoons mini semi-sweet chocolate chips.
- Stir until blended.
- Spoon mousse into the dessert bowls.
- Sprinkle each bowl with the remaining chocolate chips.
- Place the bowls into the refrigerator and refrigerate 1 hour before serving.

Serve with hot chocolate or frosty chocolate milk!

Ice Cream Cookies

Prep Time: 6 minutes
Cook Time: 0 minutes
Total time until you can eat: 1 hour and 6 minutes

What you need:

- ✓ Ice cream scoop
- ✓ Measuring cup
- ✓ Saran Wrap
- ✓ Foil
- ✓ Spoon

Ingredients:

- 1 cup vanilla ice cream
- 8 chocolate chip cookies

Directions:

- Scoop ice cream into ¼ measuring cup.
- Spoon ¼ cup ice cream onto the bottom side of the cookie.
- Top the ice cream with a cookie and gently press to spread the ice cream evenly.
- Repeat the above three steps with the remaining cookies.
- Wrap each cookie in saran wrap then with foil.
- Place the wrapped cookies in the freezer and freeze 1 hour before serving.

Eat!

Chocolate Chippers

ᘛᘚᘛᘚᘛᘚ

🍴X **24!**

Prep Time: 12 minutes
Cook Time: 20 minutes
Total time until you can eat: 34 minutes

What you need:

- ✓ Oven
- ✓ Large mixing bowl
- ✓ Cookie Sheet
- ✓ Dish Towel
- ✓ Wax Paper
- ✓ Spatula
- ✓ Spoon
- ✓ Measuring cups and spoons
- ✓ Electric mixer
- ✓ Potholders

Ingredients:

- 1/3 cup butter
- 1½ cups flour
- ½ teaspoon baking soda
- 1 teaspoon vanilla
- ¼ cup sugar
- ½ cup brown sugar

- ½ teaspoon salt
- 1/3 cup water
- 6 ounces of mini chocolate chips

Directions:

- Preheat oven to 375 degrees.
- Add butter, flour, baking soda, vanilla, sugar, brown sugar, salt, and water into the mixing bowl.
- Mix with a mixer until blended.
- Add mini chocolate chips and mix until blended.
- Using a spoon, scoop a spoonful of mixture onto the cookie sheet. Repeat to make 12 cookies.
- Place the cookie sheet into the oven and set the timer for 10 minutes.
- After 10 minutes using a potholder, remove the cookie sheet from the oven and set on another potholder. Let the cookies cool for 2 minutes.
- Lay the dishtowel flat and place on sheet of wax paper on top of the towel.
- Using the spatula, gently place each cookie on to the wax paper.
- Repeat the above six steps to make 12 more cookies.
- Turn off the oven.

Serve with frosty chocolate milk!

Chocol-Shake

Prep Time: 5 minutes
Cook Time: 0 minutes
Total time until you can eat: 5 minutes

What you need:

✓   Blender or Malt Machine
✓   Spoon
✓   Ice cream scoop
✓   Measuring cups and spoons

Ingredients:

- 1 cup vanilla ice cream
- ¼ cup milk
- 3 tablespoons Hershey's chocolate syrup
- 1 tablespoon mini semi sweet chocolate chips

Directions:

- In a blender or malt machine, add vanilla ice cream, milk, and Hershey's chocolate syrup.
- Blend until thoroughly mixed.
- Add mini semi sweet chocolate chips.
- Blend until mixed.
- Pour into a glass.

Serve with extra mini chocolate chips, whip cream, straw, and spoon!

Smootheeee

Prep Time: 5 minutes
Cook Time: 0 minutes
Total time until you can eat: 5 minutes

What you need:

✓ Blender
✓ Spoon
✓ Measuring cups and spoons
✓ Butter knife

Ingredients:

🖝 ¾ cup milk
🖝 1 6 ounce strawberry banana yogurt
🖝 1 banana
🖝 ¼ cup orange juice
🖝 2 teaspoons sugar
🖝 1 cup ice

Directions:

- Peel and cut the banana into four pieces.
- Add the milk, yogurt, banana, orange juice, sugar, and ice to the blender.
- Blend until smooth and creamy.
- Pour into two glasses.

Serve with a straw and spoon!

Your Own Dessert Recipes!

Here are pages for you to write your own breakfast recipes!

🐷 Don't forget to tell your parents or an adult that you plan to cook!

✓ For each recipe, gather all the kitchen utensils, bowls, potholders, etc. that you need for your "invention". Use the area labeled "What you need" to write down the items you gathered for the recipe.

🖋 Next, gather all the ingredients you need to make your recipe. Use the area labeled "Ingredients" to write down all the ingredients you gathered.

🍴 Finally, start cooking! After each step you take while you are cooking, write down what you just did in the area labeled "Directions".

Congratulations! You just wrote your own recipe. You just invented something!

Your Own Dessert Recipes!

Recipe Name_____

What you need
✓ _____
✓ _____
✓ _____
✓ _____
✓ _____
✓ _____
✓ _____
✓ _____

Ingredients
✐ _____
✐ _____
✐ _____
✐ _____
✐ _____
✐ _____
✐ _____
✐ _____
✐ _____
✐ _____
✐ _____

Your Own Dessert Recipes!

Directions

❧_____

❧_____

❧_____

❧_____

❧_____

❧_____

❧_____

❧_____

❧_____

❧_____

❧_____

❧_____

❧_____

❧_____

Your Own Dessert Recipes!

Recipe Name_____

What you need

✓ _____
✓ _____
✓ _____
✓ _____
✓ _____
✓ _____
✓ _____
✓ _____

Ingredients

✦ _____
✦ _____
✦ _____
✦ _____
✦ _____
✦ _____
✦ _____
✦ _____
✦ _____
✦ _____
✦ _____

Your Own Dessert Recipes!

Directions

❧_____

❧_____

❧_____

❧_____

❧_____

❧_____

❧_____

❧_____

❧_____

❧_____

❧_____

❧_____

❧_____

❧_____

❧_____

Your Own Dessert Recipes!

Recipe Name_____

What you need

✓ _____
✓ _____
✓ _____
✓ _____
✓ _____
✓ _____
✓ _____
✓ _____

Ingredients

✐ _____
✐ _____
✐ _____
✐ _____
✐ _____
✐ _____
✐ _____
✐ _____
✐ _____
✐ _____
✐ _____

Your Own Dessert Recipes!

Directions

❧_____

❧_____

❧_____

❧_____

❧_____

❧_____

❧_____

❧_____

❧_____

❧_____

❧_____

❧_____

❧_____

❧_____

❧_____

Your Own Dessert Recipes!

Recipe Name_____

What you need
✓ _____
✓ _____
✓ _____
✓ _____
✓ _____
✓ _____
✓ _____
✓ _____

Ingredients
🖋 _____
🖋 _____
🖋 _____
🖋 _____
🖋 _____
🖋 _____
🖋 _____
🖋 _____
🖋 _____
🖋 _____
🖋 _____

Your Own Dessert Recipes!

Directions

_____

_____

_____

_____

_____

_____

_____

_____

_____

_____

_____

_____

_____

_____

_____

Your Own Dessert Recipes!

Recipe Name_____

What you need

✓ _____
✓ _____
✓ _____
✓ _____
✓ _____
✓ _____
✓ _____
✓ _____

Ingredients

✦ _____
✦ _____
✦ _____
✦ _____
✦ _____
✦ _____
✦ _____
✦ _____
✦ _____
✦ _____
✦ _____

Your Own Dessert Recipes!

Directions

❧_____
❧_____
❧_____
❧_____
❧_____
❧_____
❧_____
❧_____
❧_____
❧_____
❧_____
❧_____
❧_____
❧_____
❧_____

Epilogue

I wrote this book for my sons, Taylor and Max, in order to capture fun, easy recipes of the foods they love! Taylor is experiencing the fun of cooking while Max enjoys playing with the utensils.

At an early age, I started cooking with my Mom. She taught me the basics of cooking and bought me my first cookbook. My children's cookbook was very simple and contained easy to follow recipes that I enjoyed experimenting with. I hope that my readers will benefit from this book the way I did from my first cookbook!

If you have any questions, comments, or suggestions, please contact me at Jennifer@thunderations.com.

Keep on cooking kids!

Jennifer Kingham

About the Author

Jennifer Kingham was born in Tulsa, Oklahoma and grew up in a home where cooking from scratch was the only way. She briefly lived in the Dallas Metropolitan area but was raised in Tulsa. In 1994, she graduated from a state college with a Bachelor's in Science—Management Information Systems. During college she pursued a technical career in Information Technology at a local national company and accepted a technical position with a local international company after graduation. Once Jennifer moved into her own home, she began experimenting with family recipes and eventually started creating her own. In 1999, Jennifer married Chris Kingham and became a full time step-Mom to Taylor. Jennifer and Chris expanded their family and had Max in 2001. During the last few years, she has created kid-friendly recipes that she and her sons cook together.

After twelve years of technical, project, and management positions, she needed a change! Jennifer devoted her "spare" time to writing this cookbook for her sons, Taylor and Max!

0-595-25815-8